The
Archival
Birds

Melissa Kwasny

Bear Star Press

2000

The Archival Birds

Printed in the United States of America
by Ed's Printing in Chico, CA

First Edition

10 9 8 7 6 5 4 3 2 1

Bear Star Press

185 Hollow Oak Drive
Cohasset, CA 95973
www.bearstarpress.com

Cover painting: Gennie DeWeese, *Blue Jay*, 1987,
cattlemarker on paper. Accession # 1988.029.
Yellowstone Art Museum Permanent Collection
Museum purchase with funds provided by the Montana Coal
Tax Fund

Book design: B. A. Spencer

Author photograph: Anne Appleby

Library of Congress Card Number: 00-104506
ISBN 0-9657177-6-3

Acknowledgments

Acknowledgment is made to the following publications for poems that originally appeared in them.

Acorn: "Yellow Pines," "To Sough," "After the Rain"

Estero: "Douglas Fir"

Nimrod: three sonnets from "Presence of Birds/Absence of Birds" and "Winter Fig"

Poetry Northwest: "Songbirds," "Shade," "Aspen," "An Urban Poem," "Grass," "Learning to Speak to Them," "Mountain Pool," "Snowmelt"

Rain City Review: "The Room," "Renewing the Contacts"

Red Hen Press: "Mountain Ash," "Drought"

Season of Dead Water/Poems about the Alaskan Oil Spill: "The Archival Birds"

Sonoma Mandala: "Eucalyptus," "Red Cedar," "Presence of Birds/ Absence of Birds," "Erysichthon"

tight: "Air," "Attic Birds"

Vivo: "The Origin of Music"

The author would also like to thank the Headlands Center for the Arts for the residency during which many of these poems were written.

for Anne

Table of Contents

I. The Archival Birds

I I. Erysichthon

I I I. A Talk of Trees

IV. Learning to Speak to Them

I. The Archival Birds

or like those migratory flocks
who still (they say) hover
over the lost island, Atlantis;

seeking what they once knew

~ H.D.

The Room

No one will be surprised to learn that the tower room
is the abode of a gentle young girl and that she is
haunted by the memories of an ardent ancestress.
~ Gaston Bachelard

Better I in the shadows
watching those below in the light
pulling fistfuls of leaves
from young eucalyptus. Herb-blue
and silver, those limbs could be mine,
akimbo or thin as arroyo willow
stretched in warm patches of sun.

Everything I've learned
I've learned from these windows,
how the day marches out
from first one wall, then the other.
Time passes like music,
outside me, the intricate scratching
of sorrel against sage, fennel
and hemlock locked in a tangle.
If I could touch them,
I could cook with them, or kill.

Above this room which I chose,
which I have inherited,
each planet travels
like a sleeping eye under the lid.

Much that was once common
is now secret. Three tribes
are extinct: Gabrielino,
Island, Nicoleno. At night
the ocean catches

in the arms of Spanish trees.
When the moon intrudes—
weathered the color of ancestors,
the meat of pears—
I listen less for footsteps
than for the broken bodies of kestrel,
owl, those trapped by the light
they found their way in by.

Attic Birds

It will be cool there,
the window broken
to a forest
in constant conversation with her.
She will be there alone,
the arched frame
an embrace, trimmed
in the mascot blue of missions.

The old glass distorts.
The arched frame exactly suits her.
The four panes could be
a cross she squares her body to.
One square of shame.
One of lassitude.

Although the cells
of the soldiers
have been abandoned to her,
she is not comfortable in them.

Red banners of the dead,
the endless gestures
of the living,
all colors sway before her,
those found in hollows,
the risk-taking greens.

The four panes could be
a tree she nails a cross to.
One square of hope.
One of ascendancy.

The attic shifts

with the wind, grout falls
from the brick chimney.
Kestrels, near the glass,
shoulder the blue eaves.

The Origin of Music

The far yellow hills
must seem large
to a woman walking them,
the yellow threads
sewn warm onto her feet.

There is nothing left
for the deer to eat.
They kick deep
past the maligned ground.

So much time,
there must be another life
being lived here
off the deerless trails,
the cluttered, lower
paths of our narration.

There must be a flight
between this life
we are sharing,
some thread carried
from the unhoned field
and now pushing past
the nests onto
the boards of our ceilings.

Renewing the Contacts

Marin Headlands, California

1.

Careful as those before me,
their sun-hats downcast,
humbled to each twig,
as if stepping
were like speaking
a second language,
a modest intention,
a reluctance to interfere,

(pray for rain! pray for rain!)

I am walking slow
as the old couple before me.
Paralyzed by history
and theories of natural cycle,
I am straining to hear.

(Like a bare-ribbed woman
in the last days of a fast,
a thirst so rare
the grasses seem to glow with it.)

How quickly
this has happened. The mud-
splashed willow remains uncleaned.

2.

Simple.
Say what you see.
It is there,
the green and golden wreck
under the current.

3.

What draws me to the face
in the thicket of willow
brush and reeds?
The old couple has moved on.
What stopped me? The eyes,
kabuki, the heavy
black strokes of the bones?
No sound. But this mask
of a deer, geometric,
the carving of one
who has made this its home.

Green stain on the wind.
It has known wetness.

4.

My hand slips under
my shirt as if this
were someone else's body
I am touching, the skin
salted and porcelain,
the nearness of the blue-
limbed veins. I am afraid
if I slit these wrists
nothing will come.

I am waiting for the fires
or waiting years for rain.
The planets withdraw
in their crab-like steps.
The tracks must be dark
now with such tracings.

Past history and my own
dread of loss, the deer,
its fur salted
as the hills, is signaling.

Songbirds

Oh, wives' tales, folktales,
oh, mother's helpers,
teaching the children
that the fourth day was,
that the red shoe meant
or the spilling of water,
each floor's story
in the three-story house.
Language, she said,
begins with the birds,
with word of mouth
and the pathless ways
we miss
on our way to heaven.

Birds are the first to suffer,
she said, the handsome woman
with her songbird tales,
her time to listen.
Look, she wipes her hands,
climbs a roof and sits there.
She can't help it,
she was born susceptible
to music, to grass dances,
rain cycles, thicketed rhythm,
the boreal cast across her path
like dice, like good news
or bad. And mostly, it's bad.
They come in fewer numbers.
Their speech is slurred.
She would like to be harbor
to their songs, a blue
apron, but her speech,
too, continues at a loss.

What is most dear to her
rests in the tree of us.
Over sixteen materials
in a hummingbird's nest.
Which for strength? For scent?
For air? For the rustle?
What for spirit, what for song
of the rosy finch which lands
in petals of celebration,
for the gold coin of finch luck
in the blanket toss of air,
for the thrush of arms
in perfect greeting,
for the warbler of sun
through the thick-tongued nettle,
for the vireo, matinal,
lark of clear sailing,
for the experts in herbalogy,
horse-traders in the song.

Nothing
is just gone, she said.

Archival Bird

Notice how the meat
from its bones
has shrunken and lodged
like rocks
in the elbowed roots
of a tree. Notice,
the feathers dissolve
and the eyes
become sockets
and where its wings,
still stretched,
are a relic of flight.

Presence of Birds/Absence of Birds

I.

There is melody in the place of rest.
Silence, an ancestral path of migration.
There are flyways, a ceremony of the nest
in contact through the ritual of motion.

When I talk of birds, I go back
and forth with it, casting like seeds
my country wish toward the moon, my sack
of repair, woman's lamentation: field

music, needles, the cross-stitch of flight.
Seams, correspondences, they are blue thread
on a blue robe, joining blue earth to light.

And on the fifth day, into the maimed
firmament of heaven, the air, it is said,
echoed, angelic as if from birds or rain.

2.

An echo, angelic, as if from birds or rain,
an intelligence, genetic and prone to weather
conditions, the chemical chain
of earth, sea, sea-salt, sun, the tethered

winds, the diminished starlight—I've seen it,
how it clusters above the limbs,
trembling and imbalanced, the intricate
weave ripped by passing motorists, or dim,

susceptible as a flame. To every sound,
I, too, am dim and tremulous.
I, too, am drawn to the Byzantine crowns.

There is little rest in the so-called new
world—old growth, tropical or boreal forest.
To say the body is a tree is not quite true.

3.

To say the body is a tree is not quite true.
I'm as far from claiming flesh as root,
thought a leafy dilation, voice as milieu,
wind-heavy and indigent without the throat

of sparrow—far as that grove of eucalyptus
above on the hill, a silver abstraction.
Rain stirs it and soon, the gaze between us
fills. Wind, and this wind is a fraction

of it. Not up there, but here where air is blued
by sheer insistence, my sea-breath cast
against the marine light. As I am, it, too

is ragged and warmed by the thousand warm-
blooded flocks. This much will last:
sky contains us, stretched over earth, around stem.

4.

Sky, contain us, stretched over earth, around stem,
not a heaven, but root, alluvial and veined
with the once-great boreal. Shadow-limbs
echo back to us. Even the constrained

birds come low and talk of them, their solicitude
a flight to each vanished grove. Grief
requires this, the return to what we lose.
One note and memories of each spring leaf

round me. Incurable, how the waters follow
the center fold of the blade, how the hours
shift and the eggs drop inside me. Just so,

they fall at dusk to their trees and nests.
Birds don't belong to the stars. They are ours.
Mercy would give them safe places to rest.

5.

Mercy would give them safe places to rest.
The pause-beat-pause they can't transcend,
nested as a heart, weighted as the pink breast
of my hand. With little immunity, I contend

with the hovering, the fragility, the staid
return through the delirious particles.
Song gathers from this—our frayed
disjunctive song. It recollects and then culls

from the gleam of the remaining stands.
The birds don't sing of anywhere but here.
The thousand finches skin the golden lands.

And what place gold finch in me? I long
before I lose them, gain this unbalanced ear,
because the force of not looking is so strong.

6.

Because the force of not looking is so strong,
here, inside the sun-baked architecture
of abstraction, is a lamenting woman too long
in understanding, barely cheered by the blur

through pavements of weeds or winds, the strains
of music pouring from the cracks in words
or how wrens soar between the chains
of a chain-link fence. Or perch there. Birds

depend on wayward flocks, consent of the rural
mesh, and rains which bring song north to us, fast
above ghettoized, incumbent glades to where, mural

and ascendant as any skin I have lain hands to,
it balances, held by the fields it has passed,
a breast-bone pushed against a nest of blue.

7.

Breast-bone pushed against a nest of blue-
stem, cattail, pale seeds, the threads
shadowed with drought or, whitened by rue,
even my hairs are used: what sheds

from the world finds a place here. Feather,
I say, and my hands cup and lift toward it.
Feather, I say, not without memory, the tether
of flight and that which lets me afford it,

as birds search for pools where sky is mirrored
back. Come back. It's soon a rare woman
who sings. Come back. Your absence, feared,

is bound to me as your attendance. Cup nest
or scrape, scratched in dead leaves, the ground—
where there is melody is the place of rest.

Air

Under the traffic,
the lamps, horns and bells
divining time and distance,
listen. Hidden in the long-
limbed and grassy silence,
under the waves even,
(whose violence somehow whispers to me)
the air is a tree
and when I have adjusted my sight
as I do to the dried,
many colors of shadow,
the blue papers,
the browning marshes,
the gray they rise from and dip into,
I see the birds in its limbs,
their landings and flight,
and the exchanging of places.

II. Erysichthon

adapted from Ovid's Metamorphoses

1. Erysichthon

He burned no incense, alone
or in company. The scents were
nothing to him: pine or sandalwood
suspended above our country
after each rain as basil
is suspended in a good red soup.
The time is past, he said,
for tribal fantasies, for wood nymphs,
spirits, the four directions,
gods of the Hindi or the Senegalese.
Everything on this earth,
he said, was put here for man,
the fish of the seas, the fowl of air,
and especially every tree,
(in which is the fruit of the tree)
here for me to subdue it.

> cedar of lebanon, cedar
> of the great lakes ojibway,
> laurel, celtic oak and fig,
> biblical fig, mexican fig,
> the olive and her oil
> which won athene her city,
> cottonwood for the sundance,
> lodgepole for the lodge

And so he entered the sacred grove
and in the middle was a tree
which we revered.
Our hearts were tied to it,
each by a firm thread, the leaves
veined and littering the sky
like our transparent prayers did.

giant sequoia, blue gum
eucalyptus, palm of delos,
ebony for the bowls, grove
of mangrove, teak and sour
cherry, five-fingered maple,
syrup maple for dead souls

He didn't care what we said.
He had a job to do
and no one was going to stop him.
He found the trunk,
swung the ax, and those
who spoke out were struck with it.

oak of our oracle, cedar
of our gallows, crow-fright
of the field cross, cross
of new testament, walls
of the home and leaves
of the book, funereal shade
inside the wooden flute

The tree went down in the forest,
taking much of the forest with it.

2. *Curse of the Hamadryad*

True, it was a low voice,
so low we didn't at first know
she was there, could almost
be convinced she wasn't.
Hers was the first curse,
laid like a first brick.
The bricks are ours now.
From the moment the tree fell,
the brick walls grew taller.

> *pig-haired and mud-heavy,*
> *the walnut's wooden skin*
> *and inside, the halved*
> *butterfly of revenge:*
> *these are what prayers to send*

Those of us who loved the tree
go in mourning, dressed darkly
and singing darkly, restless
in parks, pacing the evangelical
spread of the paved cities.

How easily we are disturbed.
Like leaves in a breeze,
but breeze is a summer word
and these, uncommon seasons.

Trained to hear her voice
as birds which leave the branch,
only when walking do words
now come: Punish him, she said.

3. The Earth Hears and Nods Agreement

And the red rye, the wheat,
the flame-threaded corn,
pale cabbages, the darkening
spinach and kale nodded with her.
Easy to miss
if you weren't watching for it.

4. *Famine*

They say it has a body
which it wrapped around him,
pale as grape meat,
translucent, like the fat
sucked off the bone.
They say it has a land
between the Black Sea
and the Caspian,
that it was Caucasian
and had an original home.
But this is putting a face
where there is none.

Anyone who has seen
the scar like a rope
on the throat,
the toothless in bars,
the one who paints herself
white in madness, knows:
Famine walks past them
offering nothing.

Because Earth, who can
never meet with Famine,
made a pact with Famine.
As emptiness fills a cup,
so she began her neglect.

5. The Story

We have watched for years
how nothing satisfies him,
his house and larder emptying,
his sources depleted,
how he went on
to deplete those of others.

> *something sweet*
> *rich and cool*
> *as summer clouds*
> *must be to fields*
> *something mean*
> *dazzling as sugar*

Enough to feed a city,
an army, a nation,
(for Erysichthon was a rich man)
was not enough
to quell his hunger.

> *something salt*
> *something spoon*
> *something to bite*
> *or cut with knives*
> *something young*
> *something perfumed*

He tried to ignore it,
distracting himself
with expensive entertainments,
began to collect art,
dark boys, and antiques.

Until there was nothing
left to do but sell.
He didn't need to ask her.
His daughter saw it coming.

6. *The Daughter*

When he sold her to the rich man,
she turned into a fisherman and pointed downstream.
When he sold her to the farmer,
she turned into a cow and wandered off, leading the others.
When he sold her to the merchant,
she turned into a cup he charged a witch for breaking.
When he sold her to a poor man
for half her worth and the promise of eggs weekly,
she proved so useless even he brought her back.
When he sold her to a scholar,
she turned into a poet.
When he sold her to a doctor,
she was his first incurable disease.
When he sold her to a deaf man,
she turned instantly canary
which he traded to a singer for a set of flags to hang.
She turned clumsy as chalk and as muted.

The daughter, though faithful, was no longer able to be sold.

7. *On And On It Went*

When there was nothing left,
no serpents, no leaders
with all their strength
in one finger, no rivers
or enemies of rivers,
no flames, no stones,
no change inside the story,
no trading, no selling,
only his own body,
which he seized now
with a vengeance,
he fed on his shrinking self.

It all started with the tree.
One absence led to another.

III. A Talk of Trees

What kind of times are they, when
A talk of trees is almost a crime
Because it implies silence about so many horrors.

~ Bertolt Brecht

Winter Fig

Green shadows
the upper arms of the plum.
One loud jay,
a weight, but a small weight.
I am looking for something
to bring me joy.
Too chewy and bitter for birds,
the wasting figs deflate.
One by one, belly-shaped,
they land
with the defeated. Above,
the naked folds of the trunk.
Once, the birds were used to me.
Now they hide
in their dry chambers.
It's not cold enough
for birds or green to disappear.
Only disinterest
in the deepening of all
I once owned, the drink-stained
wide experience of leaves.

Red Cedar

The scent of prayer is on my hands
from when I gathered it,
rose-red and burning
among the darker, duller limbs.
Cedar, I whisper,
and it shines from my fire-bundle.
Ladder, I think
as I gaze up through its branches.
Sweet yam of my winter camp,
smoke-tinged before the fire is lit,
not the red of sunset
but the close earth-red of animals
who can smell fresh kill
in the moon blood of women
and who circle
outside the firelight I am feeding.

Eucalyptus

Moody, they slam their buttons down
and every wind undresses them.
The ground, bright as a salad,
is covered with the racial shades
of finger-thin leaves
and the drying, antlered limbs.

Contradicting themselves
like adolescents, yet the wind moves,
a single thought among them.
A knotted thread of birds,
and a branch that screams
like a swing set, escape.

They are knee-deep in their own
broad shedding.
The bark clasps and swoons.
They cannot walk away from it.

Madrone

Animal, this nakedness, the bark
rolled back
as a bear or dog would bare its teeth.

Whose limbs, red and gold as mango,
flare like lanterns
among the darker, creek-side trees.

Glowing above the charred wrist
of root, they light
the wild iris in the muddy bottom.

They glow. They grow acrobatic,
offering their arms.
Shameless, they coil through the forest.

What is hidden inside us is suddenly
exposed to air.
The trunks gleam like a wound gleams.

Yellow Pines

Dreams come to them.
Their yellow fingers trace
the scripts of wind.
Under bark,
the secret glyph of bugs.

Their breath keeps them.
Although they sway,
they are pulled back to it.

In single concentration,
like a prayer,
they point to roundness.

They bind themselves to rock
until their weight
uproots the mountain.
Their stillness
calls forth stillness in us.

They are closer than god.
Omniscient,
yet they hold us witness.

Their dead lie among them
with rotting hearts.
No wonder they whisper.

Mountain Pines

Snow in the high country,
winter's pocket,
temple.
The pines are like the holy
on reservations
who pray
for the world
in the form of water.

All night, white-robed,
cold
pulled to their hearts.

When the sun returns
to remind them
that this heaviness
is not theirs to carry,
the shadow
of all that leaves them
passes like blue
wings between the trunks.

Cottonwood

Wagachun, the Sioux say
for the rustling leaves
of cottonwood
which die for us, which drop
one by one
like yellow finches
among the hundred green.

The sky smears as it fades
onto the gray wood
of the porch.
Tree light. Fire light.
Even at noon, it crosses us.

Everything is falling.
Birds swim through dry waves.
The leaves
point to earth
as Sioux lodges do to heaven.

They tie themselves to this tree
and now,
must dance free of it,
this tree
they have chosen, this tree
they pretend they've captured.

Elm

for Susanne

What a human breath could send
are these samaras
like drying slips of wind.

Or should I say parenthesis,
how they litter through our days
and still fall outside us.

They are shrunken wings of moths,
small, white. We missed
their fall from air's wide cloth.

Who piled them under this tree?
All that happens,
caterpillar to butterfly—you see,

the cocoon tricks us. We forget
the slow approach of light.
Curled on a rag-pile, the orchid-

body breathes like the sea breathes,
obvolute as rose petals
until one day, the muslin weave

billows, soft as a seed that lands.
It is gesture which transforms us.
The old woman unfolds her hands.

Aspen

Their respiration slows
with each shift of wind, light.
At night they doze
in the shallows. When they dream
in winter, they slide
from their cliffs to the green-
rooted lake below them.

The white trunks I love
and the far blue that grows
between them. Listen
how the wind leafs through,
looking for secret pages.

The milky trunks are dreaming,
leave their dust on my palms.
They never dream alone
but in clusters like a sonata.

Their beauty, my beauty. The air
is cleansed between us.
And color I had no eyes for,
the white green violet larkspur,
generous, porous as my skin
after sex, snows
between trunks and awakens me.

Douglas Fir

I am lucky to have found you,
your breastwork,
caught in the open-ended rain.

One bolt, one shriek of fate.
The dry grass
sizzles, the electric ground.

I am a woman who has resented
the courage in men,
that they never admit how much

they need this, someone taller,
stronger,
to whom the blows will fall.

You, who know nothing of these
wars, for whom survival
is a simpler sexual—no one stops

but me. The white rain fades,
clarifies. So, this
is what you see. A creek shuttles

past, and speeds, the slow gray
animals return.
Even the light comes unevenly.

Look how raindrops trust you,
the brilliant
pause and flutter of their wings.

You are the god I would choose,
who multiplies,
who breaks the fall of angels.

Willow

Moon thicket, shadow bundle,
grass of complicity,
little leaf of the hidden sun,
you are never alone.
Clan of the red-stemmed, gold
complexioned, a thread
of purple woven in the hood
you share as sisters;
growing beyond the thistle,
you are thin-boned, fragrant.

You imitate each other,
roots washed in a crown of light,
each one distinct,
but in similar meditation.
You are full of distractions,
yet there is no strife among you.

You absorb what you live close to,
blanket what you love,
bend over it as the cliffs bend
the sound of water breaking.

You have no eyes to close to this.
You are all ears. Thrown
like the stray moon to this path,
you follow it as it leaves you.

Lodgepole Pines

By their shadows, they are sewn
together. Gray, more twig than green.
How do they move
from melancholia without roads?

Eager, they lean into the least
breeze. The breeze is like a flame.
To be so sure
that what comes to you is yours.

For them, there is no difference
between what irritates, what inspires.
What do you have
already? When were you last happy?

No roads, no need to build them.
They stand like wrought-iron fences.
In endless amputation,
they lay their kindling down.

It is the growth that didn't take.
Black claws, these half-limbs
clamor for the ground.
The thirst, the scabs, the pillage.

Dried web of fever dreams,
they are the pyre they've been building.
Even the new limbs look stricken
as if they were already on fire.

Mountain Ash

No one, they say, knows anyone.
The rare ash
was invisible until this bare time.

Its summer words were a swirl,
forgettable.
Now they come to me as a poet's

do in sleep—singular, back-lit
and true.
Stars to steer by through the limbs.

As if the red berries were balanced
within
a calligraphy of smoke, they float

like the clothing of the drowned.
Vespertine.
To bloom when all else is fading.

When the water slows and wrinkles
into a cellophane of ice,
into sharp fins on the creek stones,

I will find it: the bark stretched so
taut it shines.
White heart, cold splash of lichen.

Here, far from fellowship, the ash
distinguishes itself
and makes of private fruit a shrine.

IV. Learning to Speak to Them

Drought

Clean and robed, I carry
in small buckets
the cloud-filled remains
of my quarter tub of water.
The garden lacks light—
only that far corner
I planted in borage
for my eyes, the wide cloths
of comfrey for my back.
The rose spines are tall,
too thin like the sick
men on our streets here,
but they continue to blossom.
Forget-me-nots huddle,
girls on a school yard
who never try their bounds.

Basho wrote of peasants
who dressed in their finest
to cross the high passes.
I check to see if the plums
are still here, if the calla
has returned from last season.
The buckets are my excuse.
Dry earth, from which so much
pushes out, is unbreakable.

An Urban Poem

What is worried inside me
has been there too long.
The knuckled purple toes
of ginger are raw
after I cut the dead stalks.
Seasonal, we live seasonally.

It is now cheaper to buy food
than to grow food.
I've had to learn
to live inside a tree's awareness.
An urban poem, they say.
A human poem is what they mean.

The way the snow-blooming plum
brushed my hair
when I passed under it,
I knew
I had not brushed against it.

There are words which have,
we say, no place
in the city—tender, garden,
finch mouth stuffed with
fluffs of blossom—we
who are so angry with each other.

Mockingbird

Bell, lever, tea whistle,
snap of the tongue, croak.
When they are gone,
it is you who remember them.

Teeth-grinder, desk-ringer,
a rotary phone.
You bring them back to us
distorted, but
look how much you practice.

Tea's done! Tea's done!
You shoot up from the branch,
land riled by the effort.

Broken bracelet, muckraker,
a stick in the spokes.
You discriminate.
The dog barks and you ignore it.

You are fluent as someone who
knows how to say only
good morning and thank you
in seven different languages.

Calling stone, crook. The cats
think you're a loud mouth.
Do you think you fool anyone?

The house finch begins.
You try to lower your pitch to his
but soon there you go,
solitary above the cedar.
Who's coming? Who's leaving?

You are trying on hats with no
intention of buying.
Everyone brings you songs.
Like a fool, you repeat
for the sheer joy of repetition.
I love you too, you say. I love you.

Trust Me

I am not like the others.
When I was born,
painted birds took flight.
Yes, I talk to my dead
though I don't listen as closely.
Birch bark, salmon,
I have been that color.
I am afraid of large dogs
and failure, or as Plath said,
of pretending to be
a better person than I am.
My first name is an herb
that sweetens
the sourness of the last.
I was born with question marks
like the poisoned
blades of roadside thistle.
I was born blue
with a thimbleful of bad air.
I have yeast under my nails.
Flowers bloom behind my lids.
When I step down
inside myself, it is past
white roots, bickering water.
There are stones
too heavy to bring up.
The yellow-green
mead of August, and asters,
I have been that color.
My name is a balm,
a honey I have seen ghosts
drift in and out of
as it ages.
What would I tell you—

how I flirt with madness,
that spool of authority,
that I hear women's voices
in the drone of the creek?
I come to you
as I come to birds and hills,
camouflaged by stillness,
moving slowly
so I don't scare you away.

Grass

What a batch!
A clash of vetch and brome,
wild pea,
the feather-fern of yarrow.

As though in a forest, the sun
sinks through
the canopy
of seedhead and foxtail to
the cool black scalp of earth.

This is their moment, the red-
ant-blossoms
flower up the stem,
the yarrow, nappy, extends
its yellow head,
starflower, small as my pupil.

Like angels in Paradise,
the grasses feed only
on themselves. Tasting light,
they are tongue
from the open mouth of root.

They build no cage for litter
of human
words, thought, music,
which catch
and float on.
Civil, they thread the openings.

They should never be separate,
this grass, this grace.
Separate,
they become speechless, a lawn.

Shade

The trunks wind their way
through it to the day,
still a secret, everything
going on without it.
Black earth between the tufts
of newly transplanted light.

It makes room for pungency,
that kindness, the snail
with her stone
and her stone-colored labia.
What survives here climbs
or eats low on the chain.

The winds bring jasmine,
touch the clover,
lift the blade bending
under the snail's weight.
Overcome, the green
plumes are carried down.

The birds rest above it.
The late green plums,
the tongues of their leaves,
perspire in the swinging light.

To Sough

Something traveling, something still.
An agreement, such as warmth is.
The consonance of rock and rivers.

All participate or none do. The song
climbs and fades
as if it found a place to rest in sun.

Stay long enough and something live
will come to you. The trees
stand like horses, flicking large ears.

Whatever this is, it approaches
and always misses.
A quiet exclamation, such as loss is.

Something is plowing ahead like a boat.
The backwash
fills and leaves the forest a shore.

After the Rain

These woods know me,
what I lost and left here,
how I gathered
red willow by the waters.

The creek fills my ears.
The forest presents its happy life,
a chickadee landing
on the high wires of pine.

After the rain, before the rain.
The pine bark black
and the clearing shadowed.

The girl who wandered,
uncertain of life, is grown now
and knows about death.

These are not the same waters
that fill the banks
of nettle, mint, and granite.
We are not the same people.

Snowmelt

I learn by going where I have to go.
~ Theodore Roethke

You must risk cold. You must feel
love again, the bright red
inhalation,
and next, the fear, the rumble.

You must stop to smell the dead
like marigolds, mustard.
Though they were once
buried, you must carry them along.

You will go deaf. There's no bird
loud enough to disprove this.
The stories, the seduction of rhyme
wash over you.
May the weak succumb and follow.

Breathstone, browbeater, you
become all of these, the spray
on the rock, stars
caught on the jagged lips of alder.

The granite boulders lift, scrape
against each other. There is
speech and
spit. There is danger, aspiration.

You are wind whipped into froth.
As you speed,
you throw light. Someone is
behind you. Someone is going under.

Mountain Pool

Olive-skinned, her eyes
are dark, but she is sleeping.
See how dreams travel
like shoals of fish under the lid.
The direction of the fish,
though varied, is steady.
The path leaves take
when they trace, retrace the wind.

These inclinations
wear away the landing,
hooved with tracks of night deer.
Where they bank, this tree.
Where they lap, the moss.
Light rafts
on these circles, waves, roses.

In granite's strong catch
grow the mud-roots of dogwood,
the false fir and the true fir
who, ignoring the granite,
draw strength from the stream.
And boulders, like cows
who come from the high ridges,
dip long faces,
crusted with black lichen.
Here they are happiest,
open to the prevailing roots.

The white spider tight-ropes
the span from bank to alder.
Rock moss is shaped like a cup.
Dragonfly, squirrel,
fern fingers trailing in water
come close
in thirst to hear it filling.

Granite

Deep-seeded, still cooling
from your gradual rise—
let the jays and water chatter.
You are done with traveling.

Only lichen, your black tweed,
spreading nebula, many-armed,
generational, takes
the shape of germs and stars.

What is your life? One giant
lung stopped breathing.
You could grow into a mountain,
sink back to the inner hearth.

To become again—what? A public
manifestation? Amalgamation
of what you once were:
shining mica, feldspar, quartz.

Do you recognize yourself?
Did Lazarus? Or are we armored
inside also from the burial
ground where we were birthed?

Under the Tree

I am drawn to catastrophe,
the pockmarked
ruined world. Step back.
The fall is still resounding.

Here, earth once coveted
her pebbles,
cave after cave
as they fell from her hands.

How ugly it is, the milk-gray
clay, the sinew
of rotting grasses.
Grave-hairs pale as turnips.

The root-mass looms above its
birth-lake, obdurate,
a few roots connected.
How far will the water travel?

It's not as deep as it would
seem, oily and sienna.
Like an open-pit mine.
A miniature flooded valley.

I could climb the tree down
to its topmost branches,
the bark, coarse-seamed,
like the jagged bolts of rivers,

an eddy where the limb grew.
The marrow is crammed
with duff, leaf,
paper, the softest vestiges,

graphite, twig. Where are you?
Can you hear me?
Your arms are still rounded.
Your fingertips were once ears.

September

Only the cone of the coneflower
like a wasp nest,
like the mud-bank of swallows,
and a hush where I walk,
dry as paper. This is when the god
falls back to expose the bones,
picked bare of flesh, the mouth
vernacular.
Turn around, the sun is sinking.
The yarrow heads are cast in bronze.
It is always the same question.
What was it like before?
I imagine the buffalo
instead of these slow cattle,
who stare blindly in my direction
and mow the bunchgrass down to stubs.
Over and over,
covering the same ground.
Before what? Before us,
we mean, wanting to have it all.
The nuthatch, the kingfisher,
the cicada are strident.
The chipmunks are quarrelsome.
The deer have turned gray.
And look how I pursue them
against their objections,
moment by moment
as they graze toward the depths.

Learning to Speak to Them

You must speak as if
to be understood is expected,
not longed for.
Let it come from you at once,
from vetch and rye,
the blue bunch wheat.
Return from
the flight of your naming.

Remember to be calm.
Birds don't sing in strong wind.
See how our hands
move away and toward us.

Ask if they will step
from the shade of invisibility,
the moss breast
and the bark of green oak.
The black-browed sparrow
keeps close to black branches.
The faded pink belly
of robin hides in morning.

Your life is like a rope.
Fling it. Be sure not to miss.
It must land
with what weight they called you.

About the Author

Melissa Kwasny is the author of two novels, *Modern Daughters and the Outlaw West* and *Trees Call for What they Need*. She spent ten years teaching with the California Poets in the Schools program in San Francisco before returning to western Montana where she now makes her home.